Because of

I'm Still Here

A Testimony of God's Love and Grace

LORI BROOKS

ISBN 979-8-88851-684-3 (Paperback)
ISBN 979-8-88851-685-0 (Digital)

All events as true and accurate as possible.

Some names have been changed to protect privacy.

Cover photo credits: James (Jimmy) Brooks, husband
of author. Photo of author looking over Jordan
Pond, in Acadia National Park, Maine.

Covenant Books
11661 Hwy 707
Murrells Inlet, SC 29576
www.covenantbooks.com

First and foremost, to God, for without Him, I would not have been here to write this book.

To my loving family and the keepers of my heart: my mother, Faye; my husband, Jimmy; daughter, Nichole; son-in-law, Tommy; mother-in-law, Rachel; and my amazing grandchildren.

To my primary care physician, Dr. Kay Kitchen, who got the ball rolling, therefore, ultimately, and undoubtedly helping save my life.

To my neurosurgeon Dr. Ricardo Hanel and his staff, to whom I had complete and utter faith in (also, without him, I would not be here to write this book).

To Dr. Kalpesh Patel, who took excellent care of me and helped lead me through the process, and to all the other physicians/staff who had a hand in my story.

To Mandy, Valerie, Karen, and Mrs. Mary, my prayer warriors and some of my biggest cheerleaders.

And last but certainly not least, to all my amazing family members and friends who prayed for me and just loved me. I am forever grateful to you all.

First and foremost, to God, for without Him, I would not have been here to write this book.

To my loving family and the keepers of my heart: my mother, Faye; my husband, Jimmy; daughter, Nichole; son-in-law, Tommy; mother-in-law, Rachel; and my amazing grandchildren.

To my primary care physician, Dr. Kay Kitchen, who got the ball rolling, therefore, ultimately, and undoubtedly helping save my life.

To my neurosurgeon Dr. Ricardo Hanel and his staff, to whom I had complete and utter faith in (also, without him, I would not be here to write this book).

To Dr. Kalpesh Patel, who took excellent care of me and helped lead me through the process, and to all the other physicians/staff who had a hand in my story.

To Mandy, Valerie, Karen, and Mrs. Mary, my prayer warriors and some of my biggest cheerleaders.

And last but certainly not least, to all my amazing family members and friends who prayed for me and just loved me. I am forever grateful to you all.

Prologue

When you see the works of God right before your eyes, you want to share them—you want to make others feel them and understand them!

From the onset of events during this time in my life to the end, I could see and feel God's hand in it all.

I have no doubt; if it wasn't for Him, I would not be here today to tell my story.

It was 4:30 p.m., the day before Thanksgiving, 2017.

The words were being spoken to me that day, but oddly, I was not fazed by them. "We've received the results from your CT scan that Dr. Kitchen ordered, and we found two things. First of all, the nodules on the side of your neck are fine. There's nothing there to be worried about. The two things we did find, however, are a cyst on your thyroid and an aneurysm in your brain." The nurse then paused, awaiting my response, at which time I did not have one, nor did I flinch or drop the phone. I'm a registered nurse, and I did know what it meant to have an aneurysm and the dangers of what can happen to you if one should start leaking or, worse yet, rupture.

I gathered my untroubled thoughts and visualized the aneurysm being in the lower part of my brain or even in my brain stem area since the scan was done of my neck. So I asked her, "Where is it located?"

She replied, "It's in your left-middle cerebral artery. If you go through your left temple and your left eye, it is approximately where the axis meets. It appears to be around five millimeters in size."

Immediately a friend of mine and fellow nurse popped into my mind, someone who actually *had* this size brain aneurysm, to which it was being "watched." I did know that if they were five millimeters or less, they were usually monitored and nothing was done to them unless they started growing in size, start to interfere with parts of the brain, begin to leak, and/or of course, rupture altogether.

After thinking about it for a few more seconds, I asked her, "How in the world did they find it with it being up that high?"

"I'm not sure" she stated back.

I thought back to the day of the scan, and I remembered that it was a student. A very sweet young lady with long brown hair. I remembered telling her, "Thank you," and telling her what a wonderful job she had done as she walked me back to the waiting room where my husband, Jimmy, was waiting for me.

Wow! Little did I know, at that time, what a *truly wonderful* job she had done. I also knew that it was with the help of God that she scanned as she did. I could just picture her hand being led upward by Him as she scanned higher than was needed that day.

Stepping back in time and to things that had happened in the previous months leading up to this point, I had no doubt *whatsoever* that God Himself had had a hand in it all. I will always believe that that's the reason I was so unfazed by the results, otherwise, I would have been petrified!

It all started on September 28 of that same year. I had a six-month routine appointment with my primary-care physician, Dr. Kay Kitchen. I was seated on the examination table, and she was doing her usual physical assessment. Everything was checking out okay until she was palpating (assessing with her fingertips) the lymph nodes on both sides of my neck. She tilted her head a bit as she rechecked the left side. I knew that I had some enlarged lymph nodes on that side, about midway down. They started out small and had grown in size over the past month or so. They were unnoticeable to the eye but could be easily felt upon palpation.

She told me that she would like to order a CT (computerized tomography) scan just to make sure it wasn't something that we needed to worry about. I agreed, so she went on to tell me that she would send over an order to our local hospital's imaging department and that they would call me to set up an appointment.

We finished up my visit, and then we both went on about our day.

On my previous appointment with her, my platelet (blood-clotting cell) levels had come back abnormally high, so she had referred me to one of our best hematologists in town. Incidentally, I had an appointment with him approximately two weeks after she had put in the order for the CT scan.

So the appointment was made with the imaging department for mid-October. About a week later, I started to notice that the nodules had been decreasing in size; therefore, it was telling me that there was really nothing there to be worried about. *But*, as I'm knowing this and acknowledging it, at the same time, I was hearing a voice inside my head saying, "*You still need to get the scan.*"

A few days later, as I was driving to my hematology appointment, I started thinking about how my visit would go. I knew that as my physician was also an oncologist, he would immediately assess/palpate the nodules as soon as I told him that Dr. Kitchen had ordered a scan. And like me, he would also know, without a single doubt, that the nodules were nothing to be worried about or anything that would need further testing.

Once he did assess them, he said, "I don't see or feel anything there to be concerned about, so if you would like to, you can cancel the scan."

I stated to him with a warm smile, "I know there's nothing *there* too, but something keeps telling me that I still need to get that scan."

He smiled back with a look of sincerity on his face and said, "*Definitely!* You always have to do what you feel like you need to do for yourself!" He, like all my other health-care providers and specialists, is a *completely amazing* physician, one whom I admire and trust 100 percent!

As more *events* continued to unfold, I was at work one day and was assisting one of our cardiophysiologists, Dr. Hamilton, with some procedures. We had just finished up a cardioversion (in which we *shock* the patient's heart to get it back into rhythm), so I decided to go to lunch before the next procedure was to begin.

As I was walking down the hallway to our break room, I stopped in my tracks. All of a sudden, I started having severe left chest pain and shortness of breath. I was almost certain that I was having a pulmonary embolism because of my high platelet levels. I went back to our nurses' station and told my coworkers what was going on. One came and took my blood pressure, which turned out to be really high. At that point, I decided to go down to the emergency center so that I could be checked out and see what was going on.

Upon arrival, they immediately ran an EKG on me and then sat me in the waiting area until we could receive the results that would help determine what steps needed to be taken next. I texted one of my friends on our unit and asked her to please get Dr. Hamilton to take a look at it and see what he thought.

He did so and then called me to let me know the results. He said that he just saw a small abnormality with the EKG and that he would be down momentarily to check on me. He also stated that he wanted a cardiac workup done on me and would like for it to be done every six hours times three sets. This consists of labs relating directly to the heart muscle. It shows if there is any muscle damage present.

Stepping back even earlier in time to the spring and summer and to when Jimmy and I traveled a good bit, I remember him always saying something about the swelling that was in my feet and lower legs. He was very concerned, but I always blew it off, saying, "I'm just gaining a little weight!" and laughed. I would also get very short of breath on exertion, but I always thought it was because I was so out of shape. (I really dislike exercising! LOL)

Well, Dr. Hamilton did come down to check on me, and he ended up wanting me to be admitted so that he could run further tests. I was fine with that. I definitely wanted to get to the bottom of what was going on.

I was checked into my room on the third floor, one of the medical/surgical units. I knew everyone who worked on this floor, as it had been my "home floor" for so many years as a nurse. I felt completely at home.

That evening, he ordered an echocardiogram, a test that would show the inner workings of my heart, the valves, and so forth.

As the echo tech arrived and was setting up his equipment Dr. Hamilton happened to walk right in. *Perfect timing*, I thought. I would not have to wait for the results. The expert was right there! The tech started scanning around my heart area, and after a few minutes, Dr. Hamilton pointed at the screen and stated with urgency, "SHE HAS DIASTOLIC DYSFUNCTION!"

The tech nodded in agreement.

Now as I said earlier, I'm a nurse and all, but I had no idea what he meant by this, or if it was something that he could *fix*.

He explained to me, "The bottom part of your heart is not relaxing to allow for the blood to pump in. It stays contracted. Therefore, the blood is being forced back out." Hence the reason for all the swelling that was going on in my lower extremities. He immediately ordered a dose of hydrochlorothiazide (HCTZ as we call it) and lisinopril for me. The HCTZ would help me rid the excess fluid from my body, and the lisinopril would help the bottom part of my heart, the ventricles, to work properly.

Over the course of the night, from eleven to six-thirty in the morning, I put out (urinated) 2,300 CCs of fluid. That's about five times the normal amount of output for anyone over that amount of time. Upon weighing myself the next morning, I had lost roughly six pounds. My body had been in extreme fluid overload, which explained the pain and shortness of breath the day before. I will follow up more on this part of the story and its importance a little later.

Stepping back up to the present. Now that I had the diagnosis of an aneurysm, it's time to figure out where to go from here, what doctors to see, and what tests/exams I need to have.

Jimmy was sitting close by, overhearing my conversation with the nurse. He had a look of disbelief and anxiousness on his face as I hung up.

I told him everything that she had said and about my friend who had the same size aneurysm and that she is okay. I tried to explain to him that everything would be okay for me as well.

I texted one of my close friends (again, a nurse) and told her what had just transpired, and she, like Jimmy, was in total disbelief. She blurted out, "You need to call Dr. Patel RIGHT NOW!"

I immediately said, "I am not going to do that! I don't know him like that!" He is our local neurologist, and she had been seeing him for quite some time for her migraines. They had a great rapport. I would accompany him to our patients' rooms from time to time for assessments and such, but I had never struck up a personal conversation with him. It was just not something that I did with the majority of the doctors on the floors on which I worked at our hospital.

So my friend and I talked for a bit longer and then hung up. Just a few minutes later, my text alert went off, and it was her, saying, "Dr. Patel said to call him RIGHT NOW! Here's his number."

I just started shaking my head, and after a couple of minutes, I went ahead and gave him a call.

He answered his phone immediately, and the first words out of his mouth were, "How did they find an aneurysm in that area if they were scanning your neck?"

I simply replied, "I'm not sure. Maybe it's because she was a student?" I think he was just so perplexed by the situation.

After that, he told me that he would be closed until Monday morning since the next day was Thanksgiving and most doctor's offices are closed for the holidays. He said that he wanted to see me at eight on Monday morning. I said, "Okay, thank you," and we hung up the phone.

That evening, I thought about who all I needed to let know about my situation. I immediately thought about my daughter and my mom and knew I didn't really want to tell either one of them until I knew all the details of what would need to be done. My daughter, Nichole, was hosting our family Thanksgiving the next day, and I knew I didn't want to say anything to her about it yet and ruin her holiday. I knew I was going to be fine. I just didn't want her to worry. If I had had an ounce of thought that I wasn't going to be okay, I would've told her immediately, like the second I got off the phone with the nurse giving me the news. But I did not want her to worry needlessly.

At times, during the holiday and the following weekend, I felt very guilty for not telling her, but my concern for her thoughts and well-being made me feel more at ease about it. I was going to see the neurologist on Monday. We could discuss it and get my plan of care/what to expect in order, and then I could tell her with some definite plans and proof that I would be okay.

Chapter 2

As Monday morning rolled around, I got up, got ready, and put on my brave face (mainly for Jimmy), and we headed to Dr. Patel's office.

They placed me in one of his exam rooms, and when he walked in, I immediately felt his calm presence. He said *hello*, shook my hand, and then turned to shake Jimmy's as he introduced himself. He then turned back to me, and I could see the look of astonishment in his eyes. He said, "I still don't know how they *found* this with a scan of your neck!"

He started telling me that everything would be okay and that he would order an MRA (magnetic resonance angiography) scan of my brain to get all the specifics of the aneurysm. The MRA is done in the same way as an MRI (magnetic resonance imaging), except it is more in depth and shows all the arteries in clear, concise images. He also stated that after that, we would know whether or not

I would need further testing, surgery, or just to be monitored. I felt fine with his plan.

Now that I knew what to expect, I could tell Nichole. She's a registered nurse as well and works at one of our local vascular surgeon's offices, so I would wait for her to get home and then go out to tell her.

Later that evening, when I knew she was home, we went out. As we entered the house, we hugged and said our hellos, then Jimmy sat down on the loveseat, and Nichole and I sat on the couch. We made small talk for a few minutes, and then I finally brought myself to tell her. I looked at her and started out with, "Well, baby, I have something to tell you. *First*, I'm going to be okay," and then I just broke down crying.

I motioned for Jimmy to finish telling her what I was trying to say, and he immediately took over. It just broke my heart *so much* to think that I was putting worry on her. I got mad at myself for not being strong enough to tell her without crying because that was going to make it even worse for her because it would make it look like *I* was worried and that I wasn't going to be okay. After he finished telling her everything, I was able to pick back up and tell her of the plans Dr. Patel had put into place.

She took it well as we were discussing it, though I was hoping that she wasn't really freaking out inside.

My son-in-law, Tommy, is a fireman and works twenty-four-hour shifts every three days. He was home and was out grilling dinner for them and my two grandchildren, Kaleb and Lexi. That made me feel better. I didn't want her to be home without a grown-up to talk to and have to ponder this all alone throughout the night.

Chapter 3

My MRA was scheduled for the following Monday.

I went in to work on Wednesday and was speaking with some of my coworkers, one of whom worked in the radiology department. I was telling her about my situation and told her that my scan was scheduled for Monday. I had braces on my teeth at the time, and she asked me, "Is it okay for you to get the scan done with your braces on?"

I said, "I guess. I'm not sure what material they're made out of, but I'm supposing that it would be fine."

She then said, "Let me check with our radiologist that reads the MRIs and see. I'll get back to you shortly. I'm thinking they will cause too much artifact."

Within about five minutes, she called me back and said, with a little bit louder-than-usual and pressing voice, "Dr. Harris, the radiologist, said you need to get those braces off today and get that MRA before the day is over!"

Gracious! What in the world? So I called my orthodontist's office, explained what was going on, and told them what needed to be done. The office manager said she would talk to the orthodontist and get back to me. In the meantime, I called Jimmy to let him know what had transpired. I told him that I was awaiting a call back from the orthodontist's office.

When they did call me back, they said that they would not be able to take my braces off today because they were completely swamped, but they could do it first thing in the morning. I called Jimmy back to let him know what they had said.

I went ahead at that time and left work. It was around lunchtime, and I was already drained with the whirlwind of new events. As I walked into the house, Jimmy met me at the door, and I proceeded to tell him that I was really tired and just wanted to lie down for a few minutes.

He could tell by the look on my face that this was the best thing for me to do right now. So I went on to our bedroom, closed the door, got into bed, and pulled the covers up over my head. I just wanted to sleep.

After a couple of hours, I woke up. I felt more refreshed and able to handle things a little easier. I called the orthodontist's office back and set up a time to go in the next day to have my braces removed.

I arrived at the orthodontist's office promptly at 9:00 a.m. I said *hello* to the receptionist, and she led me on back to a room. Dr. Woodard came in and apologized for not being able to remove my braces the day before and asked me exactly what was going on. I explained all that I knew to her and also told her that I wouldn't know the *extent* of things until I had the MRA done today. She went ahead with the removal, wished me the best, and told me to please keep her updated on what was to come.

From there, I headed to the hospital. I went into the radiology department, checked in, and had a seat. The radiologist Dr. Harris who would be reading the MRA was alerted to my arrival. Her work home base was actually in another facility across town. The MRA would be electronically sent to her, and she would then look it over and give the results.

I was called on back after about five minutes, and the nurse began getting me ready. I changed into a gown, and she placed my IV. They would be giving me contrast into my vein throughout the process of the MRA to make all the arteries and veins show up. Once they got me placed on the table, they explained that the machine was going to be very loud and asked me if I would like some headphones to listen to some music. I told them, "Yes, please." They also handed me a button that I could push if I had any problems or concerns during the scan.

They proceeded to do all that needed to be done for them to get started. One of those things was to place a brace down over my head, kind of like an open football helmet. It felt really strange. Then they placed the headphones on, and we got started. It was going to take approximately thirty minutes.

Once that was all done, they took out the IV and let me get dressed, and I headed on out to where Jimmy was. It was nearing lunchtime, so we decided to go to one of our favorites—Cracker Barrel.

We had just begun eating when my phone rang. I looked down to see one of our hospital numbers. I answered it immediately as I got up to go outside. It was Dr. Harris on the other end, and she sounded alarmed. She blurted out, "The aneurysm IS NOT five millimeters. It's thirteen millimeters! You need attention RIGHT NOW! You need to see a neurosurgeon!"

I told her that I would call Dr. Patel right away and make the proper appointments/arrangements to get seen. She again stressed the importance of doing it NOW!

We hung up, and I went back inside to tell Jimmy the news. A look of distress immediately came across his face. I reassured him that I was going to be okay. He could see by the look on *my* face that I was not worried.

We hurriedly finished up with our lunch and then headed home so I could call Dr. Patel.

As I was speaking to him, he asked me to come into his office right away.

When we arrived, we were led back to a room, and Dr. Patel soon came on in. He started out that he wanted to send me to either Emory University Hospital in Atlanta, Georgia, or the Mayo Clinic in Jacksonville, Florida.

Though both are very well known for their amazing health care, I kindly told him, "Thank you, but I have the name of the surgeon I would like to see." I handed him a piece of paper with the name of Dr. Ricardo Hanel at Baptist Hospital in Jacksonville, Florida, along with his phone number, fax number, and address on it.

He looked very surprised, so I began to explain how I had found out about this surgeon.

You see, eight months prior, a friend and coworker's daughter had suffered a *ruptured* aneurysm. She lives on the southern east coast of Georgia. During the rupture of her aneurysm, she was transported via Life Flight from Kingsland, Georgia, to Baptist Memorial in Jacksonville.

I remember that day like it was yesterday. Jimmy and I were at the movies when I received a phone call from my friend Karen. She was hysterical! She was calling to ask for prayers. She had just received a telephone call from a nurse telling her that her daughter, Valerie, had just suffered a severe brain aneurysm rupture and was currently in emergency surgery to try to repair it. She told her it was *very bad* and that she needed to get there as soon as possible to sign the consent forms in case they had to do a craniotomy and at present, they were trying to repair it by means of an angiogram and placement of coils!

I almost dropped my phone. I told her I would pray for her right now and that I would also call our coworker (and prayer angel) Mrs. Mary Keaton!

We hung up, and I immediately called her. I started bawling and could hardly get out what was going on. She was finally able to understand me, and she told me that she would go to her "prayer closet" immediately!

I prayed hard with the tears streaming down my face. My heart was breaking not only for Karen's daughter, Valerie, but also for Karen and for Valerie's two children, Will and Katelyn. She couldn't die and leave them! She just couldn't!

Though none of us knew what the outcome was to be.

I walked back into the movie theater with a heavy heart. I told Jimmy what was going on. I had never met Valerie, but I prayed for her as if I had known her all my life. I told Karen to please keep me updated. It broke my heart that she was four hours away from her. I know that drive must've been pure torture!

When she arrived at the hospital, Valerie was still in surgery—the surgery that would ultimately last for another six hours.

When it finally came to a close, it ended up being a total of ten and a half hours. Valerie was in critical condition, but she was still with us.

HALLELUJAH! It was going to be touch-and-go for the next few hours and days. We all continued to pray and thank God for sparing her life. Karen would later tell me that when she was halfway to the hospital where Valerie was, she received a phone call from the neurosurgeon himself telling her that they had to go ahead with a craniotomy without the consent forms and that she had a one-in-three chances of making it through it. That tore my heart out for her even more!

Coming back to the present story, Dr. Patel said he would go ahead and fax the referral to Dr. Hanel.

Jimmy and I came back home and awaited the call back from their office, confirming an appointment.

They called a few minutes after we arrived home and asked if we could come in on the following day (which was Friday) or Monday. I told the receptionist we were only about three hours away and that we'd be glad to come in tomorrow. The appointment was put down, so we started getting things together to go on down today, that would keep us from having to get up so early the next day and stressing about traffic and all.

I called Nichole and told her the plans.

Chapter 5

We arrived in Jacksonville late in the evening. We checked in to our hotel, which was just a couple of blocks from the hospital, and then sat out for something to eat. We also drove by the hospital just to see where it was and where we should park the next morning. My appointment was set for eleven o'clock.

We enjoyed a good dinner and then headed back to the hotel to get some much-needed rest.

The next day rolled around rather quickly. We got up early to get ready and have a bit of breakfast before going to the hospital and the doctor's office.

When we arrived, we went up to the eleventh floor and into the neurology center—Lyerly Neurosurgery.

We were welcomed warmly and handed the necessary papers to fill out and sign. Afterward, we took a seat and waited for my name to be called. It only took a few minutes, and we were ushered into Dr. Hanel's office. He soon entered the room and introduced himself as he reached out a hand to me then to Jimmy. He had such a calm and caring voice! I immediately felt I was in the right place, no question whatsoever!

I introduced myself and Jimmy and then told him this: "Last March, you and your staff saved my best friend's daughter's life. She had a ruptured aneurysm and was airlifted here from Kingsland, Georgia. You all saved her! I prayed *so hard* for her that day! And now here I sit in your office."

He simply said the word *serendipity* with a smile I will never forget. He then thanked me for the confidence I had in him and for choosing him, even though I had never met him or laid eyes on him. He knew and I knew I was in the right place.

Anytime I ever hear or think of that word, *serendipity*, I think of him.

We talked and went over the things we would need to do to see what treatment/intervention I would need. As it was Friday, we scheduled an angiogram for the following Monday morning. With this procedure, they would need to go into my femoral artery (in the crease of the top of my right leg) and go up into my brain where they would shoot in dye, all the while imaging the arteries in my brain. This would give us the exact size and placement of the aneurysm and also show if there were any more aneurysms present.

After the appointment, we left and went back to our hotel room. We made dinner plans and looked online for things to do in Jacksonville. We saw where there was going to be a Christmas special on Saturday evening down at The

Landing, a venue on the inlet where they often held concerts and such. We planned to just hang out at our hotel that evening and then get out and venture over to the event the next day.

The weekend passed quickly. Monday morning rolled around, and it was time to go get the specifics of my aneurysm.

We checked in at the neurology center. Within a few minutes, they took me back to get my procedure. I had taken care of many, many patients who had had cardiac cauterizations, so I knew more or less what to expect. One thing that I did not expect, however, was to be strapped down to the exam table. As I thought about it, though, this was going to be a little more extreme than having a cardiac cath.

They began the sedation, and I could immediately feel myself slipping off to sleep.

The next thing I know, I heard them calling my name and telling me to take a deep breath and hold it. At that precise moment, they would shoot the dye into my veins. Immediately, I saw neon-green *constellation*-type visions go across my eyes.

Had my friend, Valerie, not told me about this happening when she had her angiogram, I would have seriously freaked out! It was the strangest thing ever! They continued doing this for what seemed like an hour or two. Then it was all done.

I was in the recovery room for a good while and then was taken out to the room where we had started and to where Jimmy was waiting for me.

He began telling me about the conversation he and Dr. Hanel had had immediately after my procedure was finished. Dr. Hanel had told him that I definitely needed the surgery as soon as possible and that we would discuss it as soon as I was fully awake. He said that he had a few dates that he could schedule for me, rather soon, and would put down a definite date as soon as I could join them in the discussion. At that, Jimmy politely said, "Lori and I have already discussed it, and we want the earliest date you have available, and we want whatever surgery you think she needs done."

So the following Thursday, December 7, was put down as my surgery date.

A few minutes later, Dr. Hanel joined us and took us to his office where we could go over the findings of the angiogram and the specifics.

The aneurysm was actually measuring at precisely eleven millimeters and had numerous weaknesses or protrusions, indicating it required quick attention. Therefore, I needed to go ahead with the surgery in a very timely manner.

He told us that it was located in the *walking/talking* area of my brain and that there was a slight chance it could affect those things.

I called Nichole and went over my angiogram and the plans that were made. With her also being a nurse, she could fully understand everything I was telling her without a lot of explaining. I did not mention the possibility of it affecting my walking and/or talking abilities.

Plans were made for her to join us in Jacksonville the following Wednesday, the day before my surgery.

For the next two days, I enjoyed resting in our hotel room, drinking coffee, and watching Christmas movies on Lifetime, something I hadn't done in a very long time. Jimmy kept me supplied with snacks and food from the local restaurants. He spent a large portion of the day walking around town. He knew I needed quiet time, mainly to get all my ducks in a row, and his therapy was always to be out walking.

I enjoyed quite a bit of time on the phone with Valerie. She went over so many things that she experienced and/or remembered during her aneurysm. Things that would help me better understand and know what to expect. With her's being in a *ruptured* situation and an emergency, it would be much different from my experience, but still, some of the things she went through and was aware of would be some of the same things I would go through. I appreciated these conversations more than she will ever know!

I spent a lot of time speaking with insurance representatives going over things and getting everything in place for my surgery. And of course, speaking with representatives from the hospital getting all the plans ironed out; mainly what to do the night before my surgery and what to do the morning of the surgery before I arrived at the hospital.

I thought a lot about when I was in the hospital for my heart. Here's what I meant when I said, "I will follow up more on this part of the story and its importance a little later." I know that if that had not happened at that time, I would not have been able to have the craniotomy as soon as I did after my angiogram was done. My heart condition and fluid overload would've had to be addressed and corrected before the surgery could've taken place.

Also, while I was in the hospital for that, it just so happened that the CT scan had been scheduled for the very next day after I was checked in. So I had another opportunity to *cancel* the scan. *But there was that voice.* It was definitely not going to be canceled! So I gave the imaging department, which was in the before mentioned facility across town, a call and told them that I was actually in the hospital at that time and that I would have to call them when I got discharged to set up another appointment. Another facet to this part of the story is that I feel that if I had actually made it to that appointment on that day, there would have been a *seasoned* radiology tech and not a student doing the scan; therefore, the nodules and my neck area would have been the *only* part of my body that would have been scanned (and not my head). Students aren't there every day, just every so often. All the so-called coincidences!

Chapter 6

On Wednesday night, Nichole and her best friend, Mandy, arrived at the hotel. I was overjoyed to see them! They had both worked that day (Mandy is also a registered nurse and like a daughter to me), so their arrival was around supper time. We all went down to the hotel restaurant area and ordered burgers and fries. They were so delicious and the perfect meal for a warm evening of family time. I told them of the plans and of my appointment time for the surgery. We continued to talk and enjoy our meals. It was a very nice evening. Once we were all finished, we walked back up to our rooms, hugged, and said our goodnights.

I had to do a head-to-toe bath before I went to bed and another head-to-toe bath the following morning with specifically Dial antibacterial soap. I needed to get rid of as many germs on my body as possible. I was also to drink lots of water throughout the day to make sure I was fully hydrated for what lies ahead.

When we arrived at the hospital the next morning, I got checked in, and then we were taken to the waiting room of the OR. Not long afterward, I was taken to my pre-op room. Jimmy was allowed to accompany me while Nichole and Mandy were told to wait there and that they would be called back shortly.

Once in the pre-op room, a young nurse came in and introduced herself. She then began taking my vital signs and went over my health history and medications, making sure everything was in the computer correctly. I was asked if I did my two baths with the Dial antimicrobial soap, to which I replied, "Yes." She then proceeded to hand me two packets of antibacterial "washcloths" that I was to use over my whole body right before I donned my hospital gown, which was lying on the stretcher.

She then stepped out of the room, and I began carrying out the instructions. It took quite some time, but finally, I got finished and put my hospital gown on.

When my nurse came back into the room, she had all the supplies to start my IV. I had drunk a lot of water the day before, as instructed, so hopefully, everything would go well with the IV. Once inserted, she started my IV fluids, just normal saline that would aid in keeping me hydrated throughout the procedure and afterward. It would also aid them in giving me the medications I would need for general anesthesia and other medications. She also went ahead and placed my nasal cannula on so that when the time came for me to be placed on oxygen, I would be ready.

Once she had me all squared away, she let the anesthesiologist come in to go over his part of the process. I was informed of the risks associated with general anesthesia and asked if I still agreed to have it done. Of course, I said *yes*, and therefore, I was asked to sign the proper forms.

As he stepped out, my nurse came back in. She told me that now we just hold tight until the operating room is ready for me. While I was lying there waiting, my nurse came back in. The OR nurse was with her. She introduced herself. We talked about the procedure, and she asked me if I had any questions or concerns. I told her I did not. She then asked, "Okay! Do you mind if I say a prayer?" I think she saw my eyes light up. I wasn't expecting that *at all*. It completely made my day! I already knew I was in the right place for what I had to do. This just sealed the deal.

So we all joined hands, my regular nurse included, and she began praying a beautiful, heartfelt prayer. It was so touching.

They both stepped out, and Nichole and Mandy were brought into the room. We all sat around chatting for a while, then all of a sudden, Mandy spoke up. "Do you mind if I pray?"

I wish you could have seen the smile that came across my face! I told her I would appreciate it so much! So again, hands were joined. This young lady prayed the most beautiful prayer ever. Her voice was so clear and so firm that her faith was radiating throughout the entire room! Then just as we were all saying *amen*, another person walked into the room. It was a medium build, very beautiful African American lady, wearing a very pretty dress, and she had a hospital badge showing. She came over, touched my covered foot, and told me she was the hospital chaplain. She then said, "I came in to pray for you, but I can see it has already been taken care of." She smiled the most beautiful smile, and it is an understatement for me to say I could see clearly into her soul. I will never forget that moment. It was like she was not a person but an angel in the flesh. It made me feel good for her to see that I just had a wonderful prayer prayed over me. I believe to this day that she saw the Christianity in Mandy and knew that her prayer was sufficient. There were angels all around me that day. I believe it with my whole heart.

And so it was time. The transport personnel were here to take me to where it all happened. I hugged Jimmy, Nichole, and Mandy so tight. I told them to please not worry about me and that I would see them soon! Yes, a craniotomy is a very serious surgery, especially to have something placed inside your brain, but I had no doubts in my mind that everything was going to work out just fine.

When we arrived in the OR, I was moved over to the operating table. There were so many people on my medical team I just could not believe it! There was also technology everywhere! Huge colorful screens, medical equipment, you name it, it was there.

Dr. Hanel was at my side immediately. He smiled down at me with his warm smile and said, "Hello." He then asked me if I was ready. He could tell, even before my answer, that I was. I think he could sense my *at-ease* vibe right away. We spoke a few more words, and then he stepped away so the team could continue to prepare me for my surgery.

My primary nurse came over and started explaining a few things they needed to do. They would need to strap my arms and legs down and my head. There could *not* be any chance of movement, period. She also told me that they would need to place a Foley catheter, and that would be done after the meds had started being administered.

Things happened *very* quickly and without a hitch. Everyone in that room knew their place and their part.

The anesthesiologist was at my head. He told me that he was starting my medication. At the same time, I was being draped and covered.

Softly, I drifted off to sleep.

Chapter 7

Then I woke up. I was in a darkened room, and I heard beeping. I turned my head to the right and saw Jimmy, Nichole, and Mandy. I smiled at them, well, at least I tried to smile at them. I'm not sure if that's what came across or not. I looked at Jimmy and said, "Hey, honey." He, along with Nichole and Mandy, seemed to let out the biggest of sighs ever! They saw that I *was* okay!

I reached up to feel my head, expecting it to be fully wrapped with bandages, but all I had was a narrow strip of bandage right at my hairline. I was very nicely surprised! My hair felt hard and crisp and went in the direction away from my face. I assumed they had brushed it with a very strong antimicrobial gel to kill all the germs that might be in it before the surgery got started. It would also help keep it away from the surgical incision area.

At the very next moment, out of nowhere, I became very nauseated! I told Jimmy I was about to throw up, and he ran to me with a basin. It was so horrible! I was throwing up and heaving so hard I was worried I was going to tear something loose. Every single time I leaned forward to heave, I could hear what sounded and felt like fluid sloshing in the left side of my head where the surgery was done. Nichole went immediately and alerted the nurse, who brought in nausea medication to give me via IV. The first and second doses did nothing, so she gave me a third, which finally calmed things down. I will have to say that that was the only time during my whole procedure that I was concerned that something could go wrong. I did not lose my faith. I just thought it might cause a longer recovery time.

I was then drifting in and out of sleep for the next couple of hours. Nichole and Mandy stayed for a while longer to make sure I was going to be okay, and then they let me know they were going to head back home to their little families. We all hugged and told each other, "I love you," and they headed out. I told Jimmy to make sure that they made it home in case I was asleep. He, of course, said that he would.

I continued to doze on and off. Once, when I woke up, I reached up to my face and could tell that my left eye was almost swollen shut. I called one of the nurses in and asked her to please bring me a small icepack! As soon as she did, I placed it on my left eye with a bath cloth between it and my eye. I told her to please keep them coming for the rest of the night. I would wake up from time to time and make sure the ice was in place.

By morning, the swelling was almost gone.

That's one good thing about being a nurse. In a medical *situation*, you usually know what to do and what works for certain things or occasions.

My nausea continued to stay at bay, and my IV fluids continued to infuse. Each time my nurse came in to check on me throughout the night, she would ask me about my pain level. I would give her a number between 0 and 10, with 10 being unbearable. I was usually around a 3. I was very surprised, especially after having the particular surgery that I just had! Of course, they kept me medicated—some to keep it at bay too. They were *amazing*! My comfort and well-being were their priorities.

Chapter 8

As the next morning rolled around, I was not allowed to have anything to eat yet. I was, however, allowed to have a few sips of Sprite. They said they needed to see how I tolerated that, and then by lunch, they could give me a liquid diet, usually consisting of chicken or beef broth and Jell-O.

By the time lunch rolled around, they came in to check on me and see if I would like the broth. I told them, "Yes, and chicken, please."

When they brought it and I tasted it, it was like the best thing I had ever tasted in my life! To this day, every time I eat it, I think of that first taste after my surgery. It was heavenly!

I was only one-day post-op, and I was feeling like my old self. A little weak, but feeling pretty good nonetheless.

When I started feeling like I needed to go to the restroom, I went ahead and started taking off my heart monitor leads and asked Jimmy to come to unplug my IV pump so I could go just the few feet to the restroom. He started saying something like, "That's not a good idea," but I told him I was fine! So he came around and unplugged it, and he walked with me to the restroom. The nurse called into the room on the intercom to make sure everything was okay, and he said, "Yes, she's just going to the restroom!" Now being a nurse, I know that's a *no-no.* You *do not* get up on your own without your nurse being in the room, but I *am* a nurse, and my husband was there to help me, so I thought it was just fine. And everything did work out okay. Had I been in there by myself, I would have never gotten up without calling someone. I guess what I'm trying to say is that if any of you reading this has to have surgery, really surgery of any kind, *do not* get up without calling your nurse to come to help you.

At around 2:00 p.m., one of the physicians in the group made rounds to check in on me. He introduced himself and asked how I was doing. He could see, as he expected, that everything was coming along wonderfully! He asked me a few questions and checked my incision site, then told me that I would be able to go home the next day. When he left the room, Jimmy said, "I really don't feel comfortable with you going home so early. I'm going to check and see if they would let you stay one more night and maybe just move you to a regular floor." I wanted him to feel comfortable with the plans, so I agreed with him to see if I could stay one more night.

When the nurses made their next rounds, he mentioned this to them, to which they said they would check to see if it was okay.

Just a little while later, they came back into the room to let us know the doctors said it would be fine and that they would move me out of the intensive care unit in the morning to allow me to stay one more night on the regular medical/surgical unit. This made him feel much more at ease.

The rest of the day went well. My pain level stayed at a minimum. We watched TV, and I dozed on and off, and during my waking time, we would chat a bit.

Chapter 9

I enjoyed a second uneventful night of sleep. My pain was kept well at bay.

They advanced my diet to a soft diet, which consisted of a breakfast of scrambled eggs, orange juice, and coffee. I tolerated it very well.

After lunch, the nurses prepared to move me out of the intensive care unit to the regular medical/surgical floor.

Once there, the first thing I wanted to do was *wash* my hair and shower! LOL.

I stepped into the shower and started lathering my hair with an amazing new shampoo that I had purchased through my cousin Meghan, who was a representative for Monat. I will never forget that scent, and I still use it from time to time. It had a wonderful minty, therapeutic smell. It was so perfect for that first good hair wash! Once I was finished, I stepped out, dried myself off, and then dried my hair with a hairdryer, being careful not to point it toward my incision. I then dressed in my own pajamas. That, too, was a wonderful feeling!

Once I got settled in, Jimmy left to go pick up some lunch. I was craving something delicious from one of the little cafés downtown. There were so many good ones to choose from.

While he was gone, I relaxed on the bed, sipped some coffee, and even took a few *selfies* with my hair pulled back so my incision site and stitches could be seen. Having just gone through brain surgery a couple of days prior, I didn't think I looked too bad.

When he returned, we ate and then decided to go for a walk around the floor. There were plenty of beautiful scenes to be seen out the windows of each hallway. In one area, we could look over the bay with all the beautiful buildings and bridges. We had definitely fallen in love with Jacksonville.

We got back to my room and started to settle in for the night. It would be my last night in the hospital.

When my nurse made rounds and checked my pain level, I told her what it was, which was around two or three. I told her I would take the PO (meaning "by mouth" in nurse talk) pain meds tonight instead of IV so I would be ready to check out tomorrow.

She brought them around an hour or so later at my request, and I went ahead and took them before turning in for the night. Jimmy and I said our goodnights and then turned out the lights.

My night turned out to be horrible. I had such bad nightmares! I think it was related to the pain medication and that my body just didn't care for that particular one. I did, however, continue to take it during the day because I didn't want my pain level to get out of control.

Breakfast was brought in, and I ate just a few bites. My appetite wasn't the best that morning. I did enjoy my coffee.

Once I was finished eating, my nurse came in, checked me over, asked me how I was doing, and started going over my discharge paperwork and orders. We got all that taken care of, and then I just needed to wait for transport to come and wheel me out to the car. Jimmy went and pulled it around to the specified area. Then the transporter came in with a wheelchair to take me down.

Once I got outside and into the car, I felt like a whole different person. I remember us driving over one of the large bridges, and I looked out over the water and at the town with a feeling that I could conquer the world! It was an amazing feeling, and of course, God was at the center of it all!

Chapter 10

We got back to the hotel, which Jimmy had reserved for two more nights. He wanted to feel sure I was able to make the ride back home okay. I knew that I could've gone straight home from the hospital, but I didn't say anything. I wanted him to feel 100 percent comfortable with it. So whatever he planned, we would do.

We went up to our room and stayed for a while, and then we decided to go to town to look around at the shops a bit and go to dinner. Other than the slight discoloration around my left eye, no one could tell that I had just had brain surgery three days ago!

We enjoyed a wonderful supper at a local restaurant we hadn't tried yet. It was perfect. Once we finished, we headed back to our room to get some rest.

As I was getting ready for bed, I decided I would go ahead and take the pain medication for the night even though it had given me nightmares the night before. My pain level was at a 4, and I definitely did not want it to get out of hand while I was sleeping.

It was *not* a good idea. Just like the night before, horrible nightmares came. I tossed and turned for most of the night, going in and out of sleep.

When morning came and Jimmy woke up, I told him how my night went. I asked him to *please* pick up some extra-strength Tylenol for me that day. I didn't think I'd be getting out much, as I'd definitely need to nap today to make up for the lack of sleep the night before.

So he went out to make a grocery store and restaurant run. When he returned, I went ahead and took two of the Tylenol. And that's what I took during my recovery days after my surgery. Turns out, it worked perfectly fine.

We stayed that second night without any problems at all. So we decided we would go ahead and make the short trip back home. We packed everything up, loaded the car, and headed out. We had been there a little over two weeks, but the time seemed to pass so quickly!

As we were on our way home, I thought about how to approach my mom to tell her the real reason we were in Jacksonville for so long. For you see, I did not tell her I was having brain surgery. I knew I was going to be okay, so there was no reason to place unnecessary worry upon her. Everyone who knew I hadn't told her thought it was crazy of me, but I'm the one who *knows* my mom, and I know what heartaches and tragedies she'd been through already, some even recently. I was absolutely not about to place the unneeded worry on her.

Now (similarly to how I handled it with Nichole) if I had even an ounce of doubt that I wasn't going to be okay, I would have definitely told her. But what's the use of worry when there was nothing to be worried about?

Chapter 11

As we pulled up to my mom's apartment, I mentally prepared myself. Was she going to be mad at me? Or would she understand?

We walked in, hugged, said our hellos, then sat down to talk; she asked us how our *trip* was and did we have a good time. I looked over at Jimmy and then back at her and began, "Well, I guess I need to tell you the real reason we were in Jacksonville for so long. It wasn't a vacation. I was there to have surgery, but you can see I'm okay!" I half smiled.

She then said, "I knew something was going on. I just didn't know what!"

I proceeded to tell her what surgery I had had and why. I asked her if she wanted to see the incision, and as I started to lift my hair, she immediately said pretty loudly, "No!" I assured her that it didn't hurt and that I hardly had any pain throughout the procedure and my entire experience. She was very pleased to hear that! We then talked about it and other things that were going on, just small talk to catch up.

I was glad that was over. I felt bad keeping it from her, but that was what was best.

I was out of work for about a month or so. I was having a very hard time with my strength and stamina. I had heard, especially from Valerie, that I would have this problem after brain surgery. It's strange how certain things are affected by such surgery even if it does go phenomenally well!

Dr. Hanel made a comment in a seminar that Valerie and I both attended about a month or so after my surgery, saying, "The brain is not made or meant to be opened up to air." I'm supposing this is what causes the huge change in some of your bodily functions.

Jimmy and I started walking a mile or two every few days to try to build back my strength. It took quite some time, but I was able to restore my stamina to a seminormal state.

After my surgery, I noticed that when it was about to rain, I could always tell because I would get a "pressure" in the left side of my head, and my left eye would feel like it was bulging. Fortunately, after a couple of years, that finally dissipated.

Other "strange" little things happened from time to time. One of those was a little "clicking" noise that I would hear in my left ear. It's been almost five years since my surgery, and I still hear this from time to time. I've heard that some people do experience both of these. They're strange but not bad or painful, which is good.

When I did return to work, I was only able to work one day per week. After that day of being very busy and on my feet most of the day, it would take me two to three days to recuperate. I felt completely drained! So I continued to work only one day per week for a while until I was able to muster two.

Chapter 12

Jimmy and I were used to traveling quite a bit before my surgery, but of course, we had to put this on hold until I could build my strength back up.

He always knew that Ireland was at the top of my bucket list (for most of my life) and a place I had always dreamed of visiting. So he started laying down plans for us to do just that! He cleared it with Dr. Hanel and made sure it would be okay for me to travel by plane and be on one for up to eight hours, which was the time it would take for us to get to Dublin from Atlanta.

I was completely blown away and excited that I would *finally* get to lay eyes on and explore this beautiful country! It was a dream come true!

We decided to go and spend about two weeks during the month of July for my birthday. What better birthday present could anyone ever receive than the fulfillment of their dreams?

The planning was beyond fun! We worked on it diligently for days and days. I called Delta Airlines as they offer amazing travel packages. We had previously visited Hawaii for two weeks through one of the said all-inclusive packages. It was the easiest, most laid-back, glitch-free trip we had ever taken!

When I got them on the line, they did tell me that they didn't offer international trip packages, but they could refer me to one of their affiliates that could help us.

The name of the company that they were referring to was Cosmos. When I contacted them, they were just as amazing as Delta! They gave me all the info on their company and pointed me in the direction of their website, where I could go and choose the trip that would be best for us. They offered many different trips to Ireland with different sets of destinations within the country and so forth.

We chose a ten-day tour that would take us around the outer counties. This allowed us to visit so many of their attractions and most popular places with amazing history and sights.

We decided we would fly into Dublin a few days ahead of the tour start date so we could explore and acclimate to our surroundings and be sure to catch up on our rest so we'd be ready to enjoy our tour to the fullest!

When it came time for our trip, we were overly excited! This, as I mentioned, would be my first *real* trip after my surgery. I was definitely wondering how the pressure from the high altitude would affect me, especially after the effects I actively felt from the change in barometric pressure from oncoming storms.

So it's time for us to board the plane! We had chosen "comfort seating," which gave us more legroom and more room to let our seats back if needed. We would've really loved to sit in "first class," but we wanted to save the extra money it would have cost to use toward our actual tour.

The flight was awesome! We flew out at 8:30 p.m. Eastern time and flew north going over the eastern states. We then turned east as we got up to New Brunswick and flew over Newfoundland for the shortest distance over the open ocean. I had no problems at all with pressure. I know very little about aerodynamic science, and I'm guessing the planes are designed to keep high-altitude pressure at a minimum.

When the plane came in for a landing, what I was seeing was breathtaking! I was finally seeing firsthand this land that I had dreamed of all my life! (I will explain that at a later time.) It was beautiful. I felt completely like I was home. It was a very strange but wonderful feeling.

We exited the plane, and as we walked out off the tarmac, we noticed a gentleman holding up a sign with our names on it. We weren't expecting that! I forget the exact details of where we were to go when entering the Dublin Airport, but it wasn't to *look* for a person holding up a sign with our names on it. Nice! The gentleman introduced himself and told us he would be chauffeuring us to our hotel. *Excellent!*

During the drive to our destination for the next few nights, I took in the views; simply put, it was heavenly! I almost had to pinch myself just to make sure I wasn't dreaming (as I had literally done for so many years of my life). I took in every second with a grateful heart.

We got to our hotel, and he helped us with our luggage. We gave him a nice tip and said our goodbyes.

As we entered the hotel, we could see that it was built many years ago. It was very nice but very old, with lots of character.

We proceeded to our room, and upon entering, we noticed immediately how pretty and "homey" it was. There was a coffee pot, or, as they refer to it, a kettle, with coffee, tea, creamer/sweeteners, and mugs placed around it on a tray. We would soon learn that every hotel there has a kettle in the rooms.

The outer wall was almost all windows, one of which was opened to allow air to flow in. The curtains were sheer and cream in color. The sun was shining through, giving off a very warm feeling and also making it *feel* pretty warm in the room.

We both started looking for an air-conditioner control, but there was not one! The room wasn't air-conditioned, hence the reason the window was open. Oh, boy! LOL. I think we were both wondering how the night would go while we were trying to sleep. We were used to having it *cool* in our rooms while we slept.

We decided to freshen up a bit and then maybe go out and explore for a while.

We stopped by the hotel restaurant area on our way out for a little something to eat. As we sat there enjoying our food, we just marveled at how beautiful the hotel really was.

We were glad that we came a few days early so we could rest and gather our bearings before the tour started.

Chapter 13

At 8:00 a.m. on July 5 (my fifty-second birthday), we rolled all of our luggage out to the lobby to get ready to load our tour bus.

We were giddy with excitement to see this beautiful country!

What pulled up was a nice Mercedes-Benz bus. Wow! We'll be traveling/sightseeing in style! As we came on out and started to load, we met our bus driver and tour guide— Tony and Carmelle. Both seemed very sweet and personable. We also met our other twenty-six travel mates. They came from all over the world and from all walks of life. We learned quite a bit about almost everyone and enjoyed some great times together.

We started out heading north and were going to be going around the whole circumference of the country. As we made our way, I was soaking in every single second and loving the wonderful history and information as told by Carmelle. She was born and raised in Dublin and knew her history *very* well! We were both quite impressed.

We would be making our first stop for the night in and then would head out at 8:00 a.m. for the next day of sightseeing.

As we went along, we learned a lot about Tony and Carmelle. They fit very well together and fit very well with our group. Everything was so perfect.

About six days into our tour, we stopped over at a jewelry store called Brian de Staic Jewelry in County Kerry. It was a store that had been around for decades and was visited by many famous people, including a couple of our US presidents.

As I was shopping around, I stopped to listen to one of the clerks talk about some of their items. One, in particular, caught my eye. It was a necklace that you could have engraved with any word/name that you wanted. It would be engraved in one of their historical alphabets—the Ogham alphabet—dating back to the fourth century AD. It was one that was used on stones, and it was line marks, starting on the bottom right of the stone and going along the edge upward and to the left.

I decided that I wanted one to be my *souvenir*. So I stepped up to the counter and got in line. Everyone was having their names put on them, so I thought I'd do the same. When it was my turn, I told the young lady what I wanted and started spelling my name. "L-O-R— wait! Actually, I would like to have the word *faith* on it!" So I started spelling it out. Carmelle was standing off to the side, and she gave me a puzzled look, so once I got finished with my order, I stepped over beside her so I could fill her in as to why I changed my mind.

I started out with, "Seven months ago, I had brain surgery."

Her mouth fell open, and her eyes got wide.

I told her the story of how so many things happened beforehand and how everything fell into place. I also told her that I knew without a doubt that if God hadn't worked those miracles, I would not be here today. She listened so intently, hanging on to every word. I could see by her expressions that she could not only see but also feel the complete faith that I had in God.

We all finished up our tour and purchases at the jewelry store and then headed about a block away to enjoy a nice lunch at one of the best fish-and-chips restaurants in Ireland. They were going to deliver our purchases over to us when they were ready.

As we were finishing up, I glanced over to where Tony and Carmelle were sitting. She smiled and waved me over, holding up my jewelry bag.

As she was handing it over to me, she started telling me that she just found out that Tony had lost his sister about nine months ago to an aneurysm. My heart broke for him. I gave him a hug as I was telling him how sorry I was. He then stated that he was okay, that he knew where she was, and that she was now watching over him and the rest of their family. He also said, "She was on life support for two weeks, and we knew she wasn't coming back, so my family and I decided to end the life support."

We all talked for a while longer, and then we started gathering our things to get ready to load the bus and head on to our next destination for the night.

Those last couple of hours go to show you that you never know what's going on in someone else's life, and they have no idea what has gone on, or was going on, in yours.

During our travels on the road that day, Carmelle was doing her regular thing of telling us all about the area outside and its history as we passed by.

She then went on to ask us, "Will you all please write me a limerick within the next few days? And then I would like to read them out to everyone on our last day! Let's see who can do the best job!"

She went on to tell all the rules of writing a proper limerick. I had no idea there were so many! LOL.

They are humorous and composed of three long lines and two short lines, with certain lines rhyming.

Hmmm, I thought. *Can I write a limerick?* I decided that I would definitely give it a try! I had written poems in the past, so I should be able to handle it.

As the days went on, I tried and tried to write the said limerick. It was not happening. I wrote and rewrote, and then rewrote some more. Finally, I gave up.

On the night of the actual day that I had finally given up, I was drifting off to sleep. I started dreaming a sweet dream and suddenly awoke with some words to write down. It started with, "The love that she has for this land is more than anyone could ever understand." I quickly sat up in bed and reached for my phone so I could *pen* it down! I did so, and then I thought about it for a little longer, coming up with lines that would go nicely with it. After a while, I drifted back to sleep.

The next morning, I woke up with thoughts of the poem I had started. I was filled with excitement. I know Carmelle asked us to write a limerick, but limericks are just not me!

I brewed a cup of coffee while Jimmy continued to rest. Usually, he's the first one to rise, but not today. Today, it was me. I poured my coffee and stepped out onto our veranda. It was beautiful daybreak! We were overlooking the Irish Sea. It was a little cloudy, and sunrays were streaming through the clouds. It was a glorious morning. I had felt so close to God all during our trip, but this morning was different. The scene I was witnessing was so breathtakingly beautiful! As I sat there looking at this beautiful scene, the words just came to me. I tapped at my phone diligently, changing a few things here and there, until I was completely happy with it.

I got up and went inside to make more coffee and see if Jimmy was ready to get up so he could start helping me get our luggage together so we could put it outside the door for them to collect. Then we would go down to join everyone for breakfast.

He was just waking, so I went ahead with making the fresh coffee, and then we got everything together and sat it out in the hallway.

When we made it down to breakfast, everyone was chatting and just enjoying one another's company as they ate. We grabbed our own plates and then sat down to join them. We were all excited to see what today would bring! Every single day proved to be even more beautiful and exciting than the last, though, every day, we all just knew *that* day couldn't be topped! But they usually were, and we all just marveled!

As we went throughout the day, I would think back to my poem. I was *so* excited for Carmelle to read it and maybe share it with the group on our last day of the tour.

It was now the last day of our tour. We all had our usual breakfast together and then loaded the bus.

We continued to tour the beautiful countryside of Ireland. My eyes just could not take it in enough. I wanted to see everything and hear all about it all! Carmelle was such a great historian and overall storyteller. It had been the perfect Ireland getaway!

After we stopped and enjoyed a leisurely lunch, we boarded back and headed to the next stop. Carmelle picked up the microphone and said, "Okay, for all of you who have written a limerick, if you would please bring them up! If you would like for me to read them to the group, just let me know! I'm sure some of you have done a really good job!" She shared a beautiful smile with us all and said, "I will go ahead and start with one I wrote!" I don't remember what she had written, but I do remember it being clever and funny!

Everyone took turns taking their "writings" up to her. A few people were bringing her sheets of paper, and some were handing her their phones with what they'd written. *Everyone* had done what she'd asked and written a limerick, that is, everyone except me!

As I went up and handed her my phone, I had a smile on my face. I handed it to her and said, "I can *never* follow instructions, so instead of writing a limerick, I wrote a poem!" Then I laughed. She looked at me quizzically and let out a small laugh as well.

She had already read all the ones before me, so she went ahead and started reading mine while I was returning to my seat.

Title: For the Love That She Has for This Land by Lori Brooks

Then she went on to read the poem.

The love that she has for this land;
Is more than anyone could ever understand.
From the rolling hills to the crashing sea;
It was almost even, too much for she.

At this point, she made a brief pause and said, "Magnificent!" My heart skipped a beat! She was really liking it!

Then she continued,

> From the time that she was but just a girl;
> She had always dreamed of traveling this
> world.
> To find the land that was in her dreams;
> The land that was covered with so much
> green.
> So one day, she decided to take flight;
> And flew 'cross the sea throughout the night.
> And when the plane sat down upon the
> ground;
> She had a feeling of what she'd found.
> For it was there that she could see;
> She'd found the land that was in her dreams.
> So she'll always remember, as long as she
> can,
> This beautiful place that is called IRELAND.

"BEAUTIFUL!" she said. And to my astonishment, everyone on the bus started clapping and telling me how good it was! The compliments were just amazing, especially since I didn't expect them!

As Carmelle was handing my phone back, she said, "Oh, Lori, that was truly beautiful!" She could tell by my huge smile how happy I was that she liked it.

I graciously told her, "Thank you! As you can probably tell, it came straight from my heart!"

"Yes, I can!" she stated back, smiling profusely.

She knew in her heart what this trip meant to me through the many instances she saw how I was being affected.

One day, on one of our excursions, she witnessed me crying when we were in one of the oldest pubs in the country, one that had remained in the same family for over five hundred years.

An Irish gentleman was doing a live show for us. He was a wonderful singer, somewhere around my age. He was playing his guitar and singing numerous beautiful Irish songs, old and new.

After quite a few of those songs, he then said, "I'm going to play this one. It's one of my old favorites. It's not Irish, but I'm gonna play it anyhow."

He started picking his guitar, and I immediately recognized the song. It was "Homeward Bound" by Simon and Garfunkel. I had felt "at home" from the time our plane had sat down in this beautiful country, and now this song was being sung so beautifully by this performer.

It summed up my entire life of dreaming of visiting this place and always being "homeward bound."

My eyes immediately started tearing up. Then before I knew it, I was fully crying. This song, this pub, this singer, our group, our tour guide—it was all so overwhelmingly beautiful. I was so lost in the moment that I didn't know how I was going to recover and be able to walk out of there.

You're all going to think I'm a little crazy, I'm sure, but the feeling I had, actually as soon as I walked into this pub, was as if I'd been here before. And the strangest thing was that this was the *only* tour excursion that we didn't sign up for originally (when we planned our trip months before), as we are not into the pub scenes. We did the excursion at the spur of the moment.

And I'm so glad we did. There was just something about this place. I don't know if it was the pub itself, the land it was built on, or what. But I could feel it. The connection was overpowering.

It was a strange coincidence, too, that the pub's name was "Anne's Pub," and my middle name is Ann.

Anyhow, back to the present moment.

Everyone could not say enough good about my poetry. My day had been made! Not because of the attention but because everyone on that bus knew my feelings for this country. It was pure love.

We traveled on, and Carmelle continued to tell us the history and stories of the places that we were looking at at the time. We made a few more stops, loaded back up, and then started heading to the hotel we'd be staying at for our last night as a group.

Carmelle took the microphone so she could sum up our tour and make a few remarks, stating that she hoped that everyone enjoyed the trip to the fullest and learned all about *her* country and that we would visit again in the near future.

During her ending speech/talk, she said, "I have enjoyed you all SO VERY MUCH! You have all been so wonderful, funny, and enjoyable. This is the kind of group I just love! I do want to share this with you all." She paused for a second. "There was one person in particular on this tour who really made a difference in my life. You see, she brought back my faith in Christianity."

My heart took immediate attention. *Is she talking about me?* I wondered. *No,* I continued to think. *She has to be talking about someone else.*

Chapter 15

We pulled up to our hotel and started unloading the bus. Everyone was gathering around the hostess stand, ready to check in. Jimmy and I were in the middle of the crowd, and I could see Carmelle making her way to where we were standing. She stopped in front of us and said, "Lori, I hope you know I was talking about *you!*" She could tell from my surprised look that I didn't know for sure.

I said, "I was kind of wondering, but I didn't think it was really me!"

She smiled one of her beautiful smiles and said, "Yes, it was about you, and I want to say thank you for sharing your testimony with me. You did restore my faith, and for that, I'm forever grateful."

I gave her the biggest hug I have ever given. That was such a huge compliment, probably the best one I'd ever had in my life! My heart just swelled. God is so good—ALL THE TIME!

We talked a bit more, and then others started to chime in. They were wondering how it was possible for me to have a "testimony" that could accomplish what she said it did.

I filled a few people in just with the main facts, especially the fact that I was not scared of having brain surgery, not in the least. Because I felt God being with me and all around me the whole time.

As I stated before, you never know what someone else has been through or what they might be going through at present. No one could believe that my surgery had taken place just seven months prior. They were all really surprised that I didn't show any signs or symptoms whatsoever and that I always had the energy level of a teenager! LOL.

In closing, I hope that my story, or my "testimony," if you will, can help lead others "back to Christianity," or if you're not already a Christian, hopefully, my book will help "lead" you, in your heart, to becoming one.

May God bless you all to the fullest.

Amen.

About the Author

Lori Brooks was born and raised in the Appalachian Mountains, outside of Boone, North Carolina. She moved to South Georgia in the early '80s and now resides in Leesburg, Georgia.

She was raised in the Baptist faith in a little mountain church called Elk Knob Baptist Church.